They are silent, beautiful, fragile: they are harmless and clean; they are determined; they are graceful; they stalk nothing; they are ingenious chemists; they are symbols of innocence; they are the first butterfly we learn by name. Like the imagination, they dart from one sunlit spot to another. To the Mexicans, who call them las palomas, they are the souls of children who died during the past year, fluttering on their way to heaven.

– Diane Ackerman, The Rarest of the Rare: vanishing animals, timeless words, Random House, Inc.

Above all, I would like to thank God for all the blessings I have received toward the creation of this book. Without the blessing of my children, I would not have had the insight to write this book. Without the blessing of my husband, I would not have had the ability to produce this book. Without the blessing of my family, I would not know Him. Without the blessing of friends, I would not have met Kathy, who is the second leg of this book. Life is a gift and a blessing. Be grateful for it.-S.F.

For Eleanor Jane and whatever the future may hold.-K.W.

Text copyright © 2008 Stephanie Feuerstein
Illustrations copyright © 2008 Kathryn Wedge

All rights reserved.
No part of this book may be reproduced in any form
without written permission from the author and the illustrator.

The Monarch's Gift: A Journey Through the Life of a Monarch Butterfly
written by Stephanie Feuerstein, illustrated by Kathryn Wedge

Summary: A Monarch butterfly tests several U.S. native flowers
until it finds the one where it can leave its special gift.

ISBN 978-1-55566-412-1

Kathryn Wedge's paintings were done in acrylic on canvas.
Book design by Kathryn Wedge Fine Art and Design.
Printed in the United States.

Managed and distributed by

FIELD Press

An imprint of FIELD Edventures,
a non-profit organization
engaging the rock-skipping, frog-catching spirit.

Learn more at www.fieldedventures.org

The Monarch's Gift

A Journey Through the Life of a Monarch Butterfly

By Stephanie Feuerstein
Paintings by Kathryn Wedge

A pretty Monarch butterfly
floated through the sky
fluttering her dappled wings
as clouds went drifting by.

Looking for a place to rest
she dropped down to the ground,
landing in a field of blooms
without making a sound.

Colors, colors everywhere!
The flowers were aglow
with red and orange and yellow
too, a beautiful rainbow!

Searching for a certain flower, tasting every one; unrolling her proboscis, her special straw-like tongue.

Following the spectrum
of a rainbow's lovely light,
she sipped an Indian Paintbrush,
its petals red and bright.

Sensing with her feet
that this flower was not right,
she danced across the meadow
through a flood of orange delight.

The Butterfly-weed nectar
was sweet and tasted right
but the Honeybee upon the plant
put up an awful fight.

So she fled away from him
to a happy yellow bunch
of blooms with chocolate centers,
a Black-eyed Susan lunch!

She fluttered a bit farther
and found a small white tip
peeking out from lush green leaves,
from a Turtlehead she sipped!

Too difficult to drink from that,
she lifted up and flew
to taste a lovely Lupine,
a spike of violet-blue.

Still searching for that certain flower,
she fluttered once again
and flapped her wings in joy
to see her special friend!

Adorned in pinkish-purple blooms,
the Common Milkweed glowed
and welcomed Monarch's bright orange wings
with a warm and soft, "Hello!"

The monarch rested there a while,
happy for the break,
then sipped some sugary nectar
once she was awake.

And as the day began to dim,
the breeze gave her a lift,
but not before the Monarch left
a very special gift.

A tiny yellow egg lay
underneath a leaf,
safe from rain and sunlight,
a place of true relief.

And in return, the plant gave her
its own gift from the earth,
a wealth of food, of healthy leaves,
for the caterpillar's birth.

And every day the baby ate and grew and grew and grew!

It shed its skin for five instars, until its growth was through.

The fifth instar, it formed a "J"
and sewed a silken thread
to hang in total silence
as a chrysalis instead.

For two full weeks, bright green with gold,
the chrysalis just hung,
transforming everything inside
until its time was done.

And suddenly, one morning
as the sun was just arising,
the chrysalis split open...
a new Monarch was arriving!

She pushed out of the chrysalis
and hung there for a while,
as back and forth her wings would pump,
till they were full and dry.

And as she left her friend that day,
she turned to him to say,
"Thank you for your precious gift,"
and promptly flew away!